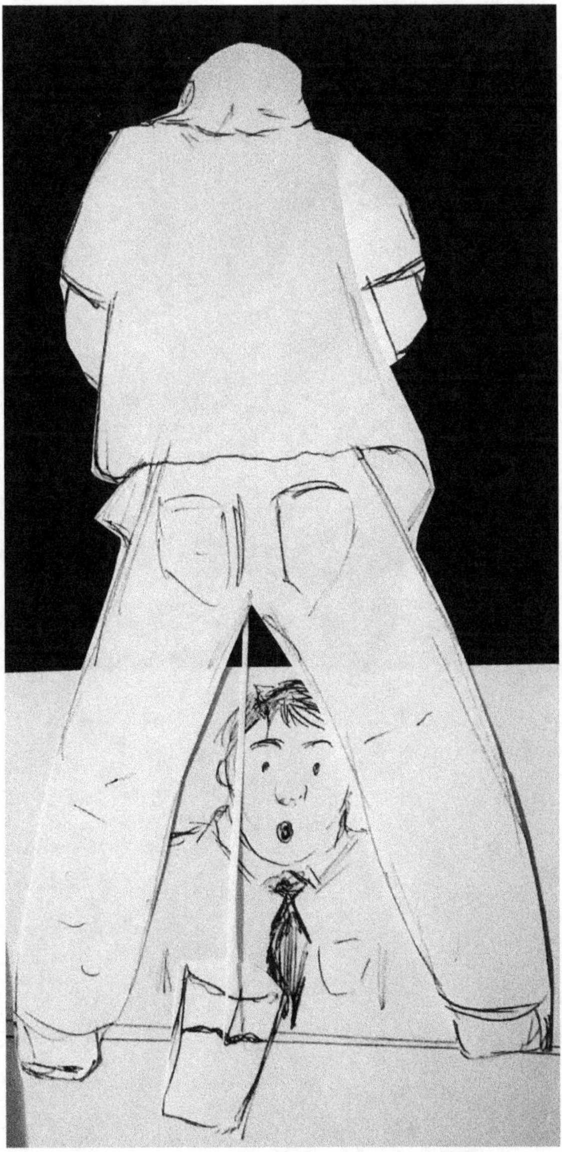

...because they said so
by w. Vincent

...BECAUSE THEY SAID SO

...because they said so

written by

w. Vincent

Edited by
J. Leyko Picciotto

Illustrations & Photography by
w. Vincent

...BECAUSE THEY SAID SO

...BECAUSE THEY SAID SO

TO THOSE WHO HAD ENOUGH

...BECAUSE THEY SAID SO

sake

don't be tempting fate
young man,
don't you know
they've been in and
out of rehab?
our lives;
our plans fill a
liquor cabinet
they cant keep their hands
out of
so
don't go dangling
the key.

do not disturb

got a room to entertain her invitation
knowing exactly what to say to give
ourselves permission.
an agreement of confidentiality, health
and safety
initial sign and date
the inner rot brought on by a
business transaction
wishing the sun never rose,
calling the front desk for a late checkout and
another bottle of such and such.
room service and door knob signs
help
those hiding under the covers
but at 33
the monsters
don't go away
that easily.

the cowardly lying son of a bitch

scattered clothes intermingling
with disgruntled beer bottles
filled with butts and
"should ofs."

books covered in white and orange
dust,
tiny bits of wisdom
coated in dead skin
cover to cover.

broken doors and bottle cap
landmines,
ants marching against
their queen,
holding signs demanding
better health care.

maybe if I cleaned up, I'd find my keys

maybe if I recycled, I'd find world peace

maybe if I vacuumed, I'd find God.

final notice

the keys on the typewriter get stuck
just like the rest of us;
the poem on the other page slowly fades
and sets behind the new

what terrible things have you done
to become such a good man?
lately
for me
that's all that's been sensible in a world
like ours.
have we all been hilariously
misunderstanding ourselves?

riding the coattails of the doors we held open;
yet never entered
the people we were kind to;
yet never took the time to know

that sensible world said
to be our stage
for all to pretend
for all to hide
for some to look up and
others inside
but didn't anyone ever tell you
all you can do is run…

the rock and a hard place to think

it wasn't long until things went to shit
helpful comments fly overhead:
shouldn't you know better?
shouldn't you believe
in yourself?
shouldn't you want to die
for something other than your own self pity?

everything selfless is suicide
passed on from enemy line
to enemy line
badges of honor
dug out of trenches,
held on to
long enough to feel satisfied;
glorified for putting their life on the dotted line.

deny… what you need, take what your given
deny… what you could be, take what's left
deny… what's right, do what your told
one day you will be allowed inside
but for now you'll have to mark time

hell
even St. Peter patiently waits
outside the pearly gates.

abducted at birth

I don't want this pain;
the sacrifice it all entails
so instead of change,
it's the shortcuts and
loopholes; the
fine print I seek.
surely there will be someone
who will sell it to me for
less than its worth and
more than they got it for.

we all participate in this game,
the game inside the game,
the game of not playing the game.
UFOs and perfect relationships, have
us all painting
our chocolate martini
cover page
lives
with more toys than we know what to play with;
middle aged and only sharing
if it looks good to do so.

have we ever really loved?
or just possessed,
afraid to lose what luck
effortlessly
gave us.

what truly can be ours
is the feeling revealed
when it's gone.

cheers

I could be at the starting line,
instead of this bar,
eagerly waiting to explode
but I linger around walking in circles, asking
peoples opinions, seeking
approval,
signing up for classes taught by
people looking for the same thing,
learning nothing;
saving face, it's
easier to laugh at the daring
than to laugh it off.
years or
decades will go by,
that permission slip will finally be signed
by the medical examiner
before he leaves for happy hour.
I'm told
the bartender gives away the bar
after eight.

so what you are really saying is...?

I need advice
tell me what I want to hear
just say it differently
so I feel my beliefs have been challenged.
tell me I'm right
tell me
I deserve to be happy,
comfort me,
say it's okay, okay?
forgive my bad behavior
I'm sleepwalking after all
I don't have excuses
I have my reasons
if you would only
listen with your heart
through the wall I built years ago,
you would finally understand, I'm special.

unanimous

controversy
a pile of discarded toys,
unfinished books,
the backdrop of today's best seller
becomes a flash in the
pan american dream.

ripples of fantasy
aimed at the aimless
being sold into the sins of our fathers
the chains that harden like a cast
hold like remorse
peeled off skin
pinned against one another
a layer of translation
where much is left
to be lost in a collection of stolen hearts
from the attention whores,
warming up to the latest catastrophe.

a temporary majority decides
on which delusion
we should be falling short of
while I flush the toilet
hoping no one notices
I didn't wash my hands.

one time, real smooth

you can't always tell the sincere
from the wicked,
the hug from the choke,
the dance from the quickie but in time,
you will see
most people are great at using
affection for
aggression.

...then comes the obituary

he never wanted her, but
he wanted something,
        anything that anyone else wanted for
him; so
he listened and
he learned to want it too and
he was happy or at least that's what
he thought.

she knew though, but
she didn't care because
she wanted something,
        everything that everybody else
appeared to want for themselves; so
she listened and
she watched and convinced herself that
she wanted it too,
she was happy or at least that's what
she thought.

and the crowd shook their head in approval
and deemed it was good.

big blind luck

it's not the hero;
it's the threshold,
the unprepared levee
about to unleash the
havoc
that will ultimately
save the dead
who wished to
Rest In Peace
but decided
to keep their tab open
for another
round or two.

the twenty percent

a cup of coffee,
stirred by last night's dirty spoon,
rests on a pile of scratch off tickets
that paid out a chicken-less dinner
one door opens
an angel bears her wings,
the waitress yells,
"sit where you like,"
thinking to myself
I'd leave this town
if a couple of gallons could get me there,
but where?
maybe the angel will drive with me from state to
state,
she would of course
have to chip in for a couple of tanks of gas
and keep her wings in the backseat
but she may fly off the deep end
once we got there.
I'm better off taking the waitress
but where?

another cup of coffee,
two fingers of scotch,
a perk, a spliff, a forgotten line in the drama
of my life
the waitress winks at me as we take off
down the road to nowhere
which some say
comes with a hefty toll
but you can get around it, if you know the right
people.

**it's not the bottle but the black bag we're
both carried in**

the bullet in my brain
tries to listen to my thoughts
to its relief a final song of gratitude plays
"...happy days, happy days, happy days."
salvation,
a final cure
the ailment and the ointment
join hands
celebrating the long painful dance.
it's over now as the warm pistol
falls to the ground
the bullet listens on
as the paramedics run in,
talking about vacationing in greece,
how beautiful the beaches are;
how affordable it's all become
and "look at this poor bastard,
does he look familiar to you?"
"looks like every other poor bastard
who was looking for the familiar."
only the bullet knew that;
hoping his little secret
was worth enough
to pay his own way
to mykonos.

a final victory

one day I'll either be dead or old,
on a journey to cleanse my "palette"
of the life I lived.
my memories will surface as absurd dreams;
my written words will appear foreign to me,
as if composed by the hands of a stranger,
moments that I'll hopefully enjoy;
maybe even come to admire
but most likely scoff at
claiming I could've done better and
yelling "hack!"

if he
only knew
the regrets
we made together.

vicariously through each other

she was one of those
days
you would start
only to finish,
no beauty
no connection
no lunch plans between us,
a race to the end
intentionally avoiding
the mirror hung
on the wall while
trying not to
piss on the seat.

thankfully I left
my shoes on.

house sitting

And so
as I read by the fire,
drinking from a twist off wine bottle,
I noticed a figure
walking towards me
through smoke and flame,
only to vanish thereafter.

a bottle and a chapter later,
I decided if it happens again,
I'll begin to worry
but I had been worrying
only without a focus.

I rang my friend to see if there was anything to
worry about,
and he assured me "the morning paper
would have a better answer than another bottle
of my vintage wine!"
he hung up and I was alone again (hopefully)
left to conjure up some completely rational,
tangible,
metaphysical explanation.

vintage my ass,
it didn't even have a cork to pull but
wait a minute, wait just a darn second.

my bathroom floor did try to kill me today,
how could it still be wet? I haven't showered in
weeks.
there must be a psychopathic leak on the loose.

I ran to the wine cellar and got another "vintage"
bottle;
when I returned
so did the dark figure,
maybe he had the answers,
to my aquatic slayer.
"glass of wine?" I asked.
"depends on the year," he said
"2019."
"varietal?" he asked
"cabernet."
although not pleased,
he poured us both a glass
and we sat by the fire.
we talked books, politics, and wine.
I admired his bravery,
walking in and out of the fire,
without purpose.

devils play prestissimo

you can choose to live your life either
drinking
fighting
loving
fucking
losing
winning for a short run followed by
a lot more losing
taking chances
failing
going out on limbs
yelling at god or
you can do nothing and
quietly take it in the ass.

room share

your vegan roommate,
shoving their lifestyle
and kale
down your throat while
riding a bicycle to
another protest they
don't fully understand
yet while somehow still
"saving the world."
where would the rest of us
be without them?

worse, or
better off?
let's give them the right of way,
just in case.

more importantly,
who came in my hat?
it smells like cabbage.

and whose dishes are these?
someone left the faucet running.

rally in bushwick

let's be different
for the sake of significance,
grow out the beard,
pick a cause, any cause and
any pit stained t-shirt.

let's not say what we mean
for the sake of the collective denial,
no worries;
you're fine
just
the way you are.

let's get offended
for the sake of our entitlement,
this space
isn't as safe
as advertised.

or let's take a chance
for the sake of our earthquaked
common ground;
look inward;
eat, drink, and dance
hand in hand
as the gods turn to stone
and fall from the sky.

a full house sold on a buyer's market

hoarders of moments
once lived
never letting go

our ideas
our memories
our mistakes

reruns
black and white films

bring me
the comfort of eternal life.

crooked blue feet

people will take you
at your word
and later home with
them

sometimes out of pity, but
most of the time out of luck
or convenience;

and you will selfishly
forget to give them
a five star rating.

are we so fucked that we can't see
we are addicted to
what could be,
what might have been?

walking around miserable,
gazing down
a bottle,
a shirt,
at our own crooked
blue feet?

luckily the laughing tracks
and applause signs
guide us through
the awkward moments.

working late

if
you drink enough whiskey
it may cover up the
lapse of judgment;
explain the lost time
and you can go on thinking
she doesn't know but
they always know
what to say
to make you feel guilty
like "hello honey,
how was your day?"

the rapture of the narcissistic dream

that's life
lady luck in bed with mother nature
father time fucking his 12 o'clock appointment
and then there's the people,
the expendable integers
at the mercy of it all
unable to do anything
except take it out on one other

with their self placed meanings
that misdirect
misfire
mistake
ever so accurately.

will they ever find reprieve
from the great big puppet show
that plays every hour
on the hour
at the insane asylum?

About the book

"...BECAUSE THEY SAID SO," is the first collection of poems written by actor and screenwriter Walter Vincent that explores the idiosyncrasies, hypocrisies and addictions that make up this existential "dramedy" that defines our human condition.

About the Author

WALTER VINCENT, is an actor, screenwriter and singer/songwriter. His work dives in and out of the world of nihilism, existentialism and addiction as well the mourning of things lost. He is currently working on his collection of short stories, entitled "From Shits to Giggles," which will be released at the end of 2021 and his novel, "Pura Vida" is set to be released in 2022. He lives in Brooklyn, NY.

...BECAUSE THEY SAID SO

...BECAUSE THEY SAID SO